Master Excel:

Primary Interactions with the Excel

Thomas Clayton

ISBN: 153300160X
ISBN-13: 978-1533001603

Primary Interactions with the Excel

Table of Contents

Introduction

I want to thank you and congratulate you for purchasing *Master Excel: Primary Interactions with the Excel.* Microsoft Excel is one of the most commonly neglected programs that nearly everyone owns or has access to. By purchasing this book, you are now on your way to saving time and energy by easily completing a wide variety of common tasks with the help of this ubiquitous program. As you begin to work with Excel regularly there are a number of actions and required steps that may seem strange or even arcane at first. It is important to persevere, however, as proper Excel use is a skill, which means that like any other skill the only way to improve is to practice as frequently and repeatedly as possible.

This book contains proven steps and strategies designed to ensure you get the most out of every interaction you have with Excel. Inside you will learn the basic purposes of the program and how it can help you be more effective in a number of different ways. From there you will learn about the primary ways to interact with Excel, how to sort and filter complex data, how to use formulas and functions effectively, how to print and create graphs and how to understand common error messages and how to avoid them.

Thanks again for purchasing this book, I hope you enjoy it!

Lesson 1

Understanding Excel

Once you understand what is required, using Excel can provide you a wide variety of options when it comes to working with data in a multitude of forms. One of the primary ways to use Excel is most often associated with the financial sector and allows the user to create their own formulas and then use them to calculate everything from an annual report to a simple sales forecast. It can also be used for a variety of tracking and organizational purposes such as creating status reports, contact lists, invoicing and nearly anything else you could ever need. It can also come in handy when it comes to dealing with large sets of complex numbers which may require charting, graphing or statistical analysis.

Excel groups related data into workbooks with each workbook then containing numerous worksheets dedicated to specific tasks and functions. Each workbook and worksheet is completely customizable and can be interacted with and manipulated in a number of ways. Data is stored in a mixture of vertical and horizontal rows with each row and column then being broken down even further into individual cells. Get used to the cells, they are the primary method of interacting with the spreadsheet. Each cell can store either letters or numbers but it is best to generally stick with one or the other as many sorting functions can only search for one type of character at a time.

Each cell can then be attached to additional cells through the use of what are known as formulas. Formulas can be created on the fly or users have the option of applying numerous formulas that come premade. Preprogrammed formulas include things like finding the standard deviation, common mathematical formulas and even calculate interest payments. Each cell also has the ability to use a formula and then display the results based on a variety of criteria. Cells can also be colored uniquely as well as given unique fonts, borders and more.

When it comes to creating charts and graphs, Excel offers up many more options than a simple word processing program can. Excel can translate data into a wide variety of form from a diverse multipoint pivot chart to the classic pie chart, if you know where to look, Excel does it all.

This also makes Excel a natural choice when you are looking to identify trends in what may otherwise seem like meaningless data. It also makes a numerous additional variables much easier to view on the fly. The easy ability you will have when it comes to manipulating variables will make predicting future patterns easier than you ever thought possible.

This is in part because of the way that you can use Excel to bring disparate points of data together through the use of workbooks and interconnected worksheets. Essentially, what it all boils down to is that if you are not regularly using a spreadsheet to make your life easier, you are working harder, not smarter.

Lesson 2

Primary Interactions with the Excel

When you first start up Excel, you most likely opened up a new worksheet. This new worksheet automatically spawns a new workbook and two additional worksheets for you to switch between, specifics for worksheet management will be discussed later. On the new worksheet screen you will notice that the columns are labeled A, B, C etc. while the rows are labeled 1, 2, 3, 4, etc. Combing the two for a specific cell gives that cell its unique cell reference. Cell references can then be used to indicate to other cells that they need to refer back to the cell with that specific reference. This is what is known as a formula and a basic example is written thusly: =B4+A9

A cell's individual reference is always listed in what is known as the Name Box when that cell is selected. The name box can be found in the top left of the screen, directly below the Home Tab. To the immediate right of the name box is what is known as the Formula Bar. If the selected cell contains information, it will be displayed in the formula bar.

Interacting with cells
Choosing cells
- You can select individual cells by left clicking on them with your mouse or by using the arrow keys.

- If you push the ENTER key the cell directly beneath the cell which is currently selected will become selected. This can be changed by selecting the File tab, then choosing Options and Advanced Options. From there, choose Edit and then the option labeled Enter Move Selection, this will let you determine what direction the selection cursor will move when ENTER is pressed.

- Pressing the TAB key will select the cell to the right of the cell which is currently selected.

- If you wish to select an entirety of a column or row, left click on the row or column in question.

- If you wish to select a group of cells that are next to one another, left click on the first cell you wish to select and drag the cursor to the final cell you wish to select. The selected cells will be shown in black.

- If you wish to select a group of cells that are not next to one another, left click on the first cell you wish to select while at the same time holding down the CTRL key, click on each cell you wish to select while continuing to hold down the CTRL key.

- If you wish to select the entirety of the current worksheet, click on the space between the label for A and the label for 1.

Adding information to cells
- Information can be added to any cell by simply left clicking on it and then entering the required data.

- You can edit the data in any cell by first selecting the cell and then editing the information in the formula bar. Clicking on a different cell or pressing the ENTER key will save the changes.

- If you wish to edit the information in a given cell in the cell directly, simply double click the left mouse button to show the entirety of the data. This can also be accomplished by left clicking once and then pressing the F2 key.

Copying information between cells

- If you wish to copy the data from a cell to the cell or cells below it, simply select the cell with the required data as well as the cell below it and press the CTRL key in conjunction with the D key.

- If you wish to copy the data from a cell to the cell or cells to the left of it simply select the cell with the required data as well as the cell or cells to the left of it and pressing the CTRL key in conjunction with the R key.

- In addition to these handy time savers, the information in any cell can be added to any other cell with the use of what is known as the Fill Handle. Start by selecting the cell with the data to be copied before moving your cursor to the lower right corner of the cell until the cursor changes shape. Now simply select the cell or cells that the data should be copied to.

- If the data to be copied is either one in a series, a unit of time or a date the fill option will include the next logical part of the sequence in each subsequent cell. For example, using the fill option on a cell filled with Monday would make the next box Tuesday, then Wednesday etc.

- To copy a cell and all of its data completely, select the cell in question before right-clicking on it and selecting the copy option. The cut option and the paste option will also work as expected.

Adding a date or time to a cell

- Start by selecting the cell you wish to add data to

- To include a specific date, add the date to the cell as either 1/2/33 or 1-Feb-1933.

- To enter a specific time in the second half of the day write it as 1:00 p as Excel assumes times all times are A.M. unless told otherwise.

- The current time and date can be added to any cell by pressing the SHIFT key in conjunction with the CTRL key and the SEMICOLON key.

- To make a specific cell always display the current time add NOW to it and press enter.

- To make a specific cell always display the current date type TODAY and press enter.

- To determine the default way the time and date are determined press the SHIFT key in conjunction with the CTRL key and the 2 key to bring up the Regional and Languages menu and select the settings you prefer.

Set cells to always modify entered data
- Select the File tab and the Options menu before choosing the Advanced option.

- The Editing option will allow you to determine how many decimal points are shown per cell.

- The Places option determines the number of places that are shown, a positive number indicates more places, a negative number indicates fewer places. For example, if you entered a 2 into the places box, typing the number 124 would result in 1.24 being displayed.

Enter numbers in cells in sequence
- Start by adding a number to the first cell in the eventual range.

- Add the second number into the next cell in the sequence.

- Select both cells before choosing the fill handle option and dragging the handle to cover the number of cells that will encompass the sequence.

- Release the mouse and the cells should populate automatically.

Add columns and rows

- Columns and rows can be added to a worksheet by right clicking on the letter or number to the right or below of where you want the new column or row to be. New columns are always created to the left of the original and new rows are always created above the original. After adding one, more can be added by simply pressing the F4 key.

- Columns and rows can be deleted from a worksheet by right clicking on the letter or number of the column or row and selecting the delete option. Multiple columns and rows can be deleted by selecting the first and then dragging the cursor to the last. Multiple individual columns or rows can be deleted be holding down the CTRL key before clicking the delete option.

- If you wish to ensure a particular column or row is always visible, even when moving to other parts of a workbook, activate what is known as the Freezing feature. Start by selecting the column or row to the right of the column or below the row you wish to freeze. Choose the View tab and select the Freeze Pane option. You can unfreeze things the same way. This option will also let you freeze the first row or column currently visible without having to select it first.

- Columns and rows can be resized manually by clicking and dragging individual column labels as needed.

- To manually make a column or row the size of the largest cell of data in the row or column simply left click twice on the right side of the column or row header.

Formatting cells

Keep in mind that in instances where formatting of cells changes the visible value of what is displayed in the cell, the true value will be used for formula references. To access the formatting options for a cell or set of cells, select them and then right click and choose the Format Cells option.

The number tab: When you open the Format Cells option you will be greeted with the Numbers Tab which provides you with the opportunity to change how numbers in cells are displayed. You can alter how written numbers are displayed, the number of decimal places shown, how fractions are displayed, how percentages are displayed, how time and dates are displayed, how currency is displayed as well as how monetary units are displayed.

Be aware, formatting a cell for a specific type of numerical data will ensure that any other type of information entered into that cell will not be allowed or will be deleted once it has been entered. If you find you are unable to enter data into a cell, choose the format cell option and reset the cell to the default General option, you will need to reenter the data in question.

Alignment: The alignment tab under the Format Cell option is used to determine how the cell will reflect data that is entered. There are specific options to determine the orientation of text as well as its direction, indention and text wrapping options. You will also find the option to shrink text so it is completely visible in the specified cell. Finally, you will find the option to merge a group of cells so that all of the selected cells are considered a single cell. The option to unmerge cells can be found in the same place.

Font: The Font Tab contains the same options commonly found in word processing programs. You will have the option to modify the font used in the selected cell, change the style, size and color. If you are interested in adding additional effects to the data in the cells, those options are also available.

Border: The border tab provides you with the opportunity to visually differentiate individual cells with a wide variety of colors, the result will outline the selected cell or cells. The Style option will determine what the resulting border will look like, and the Color option will set the color. The remaining options are dedicated to determining which parts of the border are visible. It is important to always select the options on the left before choosing the specifics on the right.

Fill: The Fill Tab provides you with several opportunities in regards to choosing the background color of the selected cell or cells. Numerous pattern styles are also available as are additional options regarding multiple colors and shading options.

Protection: The final tab relates to protection and determines if specific cells are locked or are not visible to formulas. Individual cell options will not activate until protection for the worksheet has been turned on.

Worksheets
Working with multiple spreadsheets

- The option to switch between spreadsheets can be found at the bottom of the spreadsheet where it says Sheet 1.

- Additional sheets can be added by simply pressing the plus button next to the Sheet 1 button.

- Right clicking on Sheet 1 will bring up a list of options including renaming it, inserting new sheets (added to the left of the current worksheet) and deleting the worksheet.

- Worksheets can be repositioned in the same workbook by simply left clicking on the sheet you wish to move and dragging it to the desired location.

- Right clicking on a worksheet and selecting the move or copy option will allow you to then paste it into a different workbook. The resulting menu will allow you to choose all the specifics regarding which book it will be moved to and where in the order it will be placed.

- Right clicking on your desired worksheet will also provide you with the opportunity to lock a spreadsheet. Choose this option if you wish to close the specific worksheet to modification by others. You will be offered the opportunity to create a password when you select this option.

Editing multiple worksheets at once
- To edit multiple worksheets at once, start by selecting one of the worksheets using the tabs at the bottom of the screen.

- After selecting the first sheet, hold down the CTRL key before selecting additional sheet.

- Right clicking will then bring up all the options which are available to multiple sheets at once.

Entering data on multiple worksheets simultaneously
- Start by selecting the first worksheet you want to add the data to, followed by the desired cell.

- Click and drag to include additional cells on the same worksheet.

- Hold down the CTRL key and select the next worksheet and then click a desired cell and drag.

- Select the first cell to enter the data into and enter the data.

- Pressing the tab key should copy the data to the next cell. Continue as needed

Saving
Workbooks can be saved in a wide variety of file formats depending on several specific needs. If you find yourself in need of changing how a specific workbook is saved, start by choosing the Save As option found underneath the File tab. This will allow you to change the name of the original file so that the change doesn't affect it as well. The Save As Type option will provide you with a list of available extensions such as ODS, EXPS, PDF, XLA, XLAM, SLX, DIF, PRN, CSV, TXT, XLT, XLTM, XLTX, HTML, HTM, MHTML, MHT, XLM, XLS, XLSB, XLSM and XLSX.

Conclusion

Thank you again for purchasing this book! I hope it was able to help provide you with everything you need in order make the most out of the spreadsheet program that has most likely been on your computer for years. Excel can do almost anything you can possibly imagine; you just need to know how to set it in motion. While it may seem difficult at first, with practice everything that initially takes hour will someday be finished in what just seems like seconds.

The next step is to stop reading already and start practicing. Remember, using Excel properly is a skill, and like any other skill it needs to be used regularly if you ever hope to improve.

Finally, if you enjoyed this book, then I'd like to ask you for a favor, would you be kind enough to leave a review for this book on Amazon? It'd be greatly appreciated!

Next Book #2:

All About Formulas and Functions

- **Lesson 3: Sorting and Filtering Data**
- **Lesson 4: All About Formulas and Functions**

http://www.amazon.com/dp/B01EVVH4CU

When looking for the type of job that will help you get ahead in the world, one reoccurring skills gets asked about time, after time, after time. Despite the prevalence of spreadsheet software on every business computer for nearly 30 years, many people are still confounded when it comes to even completing basics tasks in Microsoft Excel. If you are tired of working harder, not smarter, then Excel for Everyone: The Simplest Way to Enter the Rich World of the Calc Spreadsheet is the book you have been waiting for.

This book is written for those who have heard about Excel and how useful it is for years, if not decades and are finally ready to take the plunge and learn everything there is to know about Excel basics. It describes everything you need to know when it comes to understanding what Excel is for and when to use it for the best results.

What's more, there is plenty of information on how to go about using Excel to enter complicated formulas and solve them automatically, so you don't have too. You will also learn how to share your work with others in the easiest and most concise way possible, by letting Excel automatically graph the data you have entered in dozens of different ways. Save yourself countless hours of frustration coupled with limited results, pick up this book today.

Inside you will find

- Everything you need to make Excel work for you
- A complete breakdown of the Excel interface and system
- Common error messages, what they mean and how to fix them
- Surefire tips to make the most out of built-in functions
- Detailed explanations of every type of chart imaginable and what they're best at
- Easy ways to create tables and export them anywhere

And more…

Other Book:

#1 Primary Interactions with the Excel

- Lesson 1: Understanding Excel
- Lesson 2: Primary Interactions with the Excel

http://www.amazon.com/dp/B01EVUW23W

#2 All About Formulas and Functions

- Lesson 3: Sorting and Filtering Data
- Lesson 4: All About Formulas and Functions

http://www.amazon.com/dp/B01EVVH4CU

#3 Sharing Your Work, Charts and Graphing

- Lesson 5: Sharing Your Work
- Lesson 6: Error Messages and Bonus Tips

http://www.amazon.com/dp/B01EVX5YA2

#4 Data Validation Functioning and Conditional Formulas

- Lesson 7: Data Validation Functioning
- Lesson 8: Conditional Formulas

http://www.amazon.com/dp/B01EVYCXLY

#5 Matrixal Functions and Vertical Lookup

- Lesson 9: Matrixal Functions
- Lesson 10: Vertical Lookup/Horizontal Lookup

http://www.amazon.com/dp/B01EVYURV2

#6 Management of the Name Box and Filters

- Lesson 11: Management of the Name Box
- Lesson 12: Filters

http://www.amazon.com/dp/B01EVZBPMG

#7 Pivot Tables and Make the Most of Macros

- Lesson 13: Pivot Tables
- Lesson 14: Make the Most of Macros

http://www.amazon.com/dp/B01EVZS45C

#8 Modeling Management and Power View

- Lesson 15: Modeling Management
- Lesson 16: Power View

http://www.amazon.com/dp/B01EW0BG88

www.ingramcontent.com/pod-product-compliance
Lightning Source LLC
Chambersburg PA
CBHW052143070326
40690CB00047B/2050